MY GRAND

By Farina Leong

illustrated by Michelle Angela

For Riley & Ashley

First published 2025
Copyright © Farina Leong 2025

All rights reserved. No part of this publication may be reproduced or transmitted in any form or by any means, electronic, or mechanical, including photocopying, recording, or by any information storage and retrieval system, without permission in writing from the copyright owner.

ISBN: 9798308052456

Written by Farina Leong
Illustrated by Michelle Angela

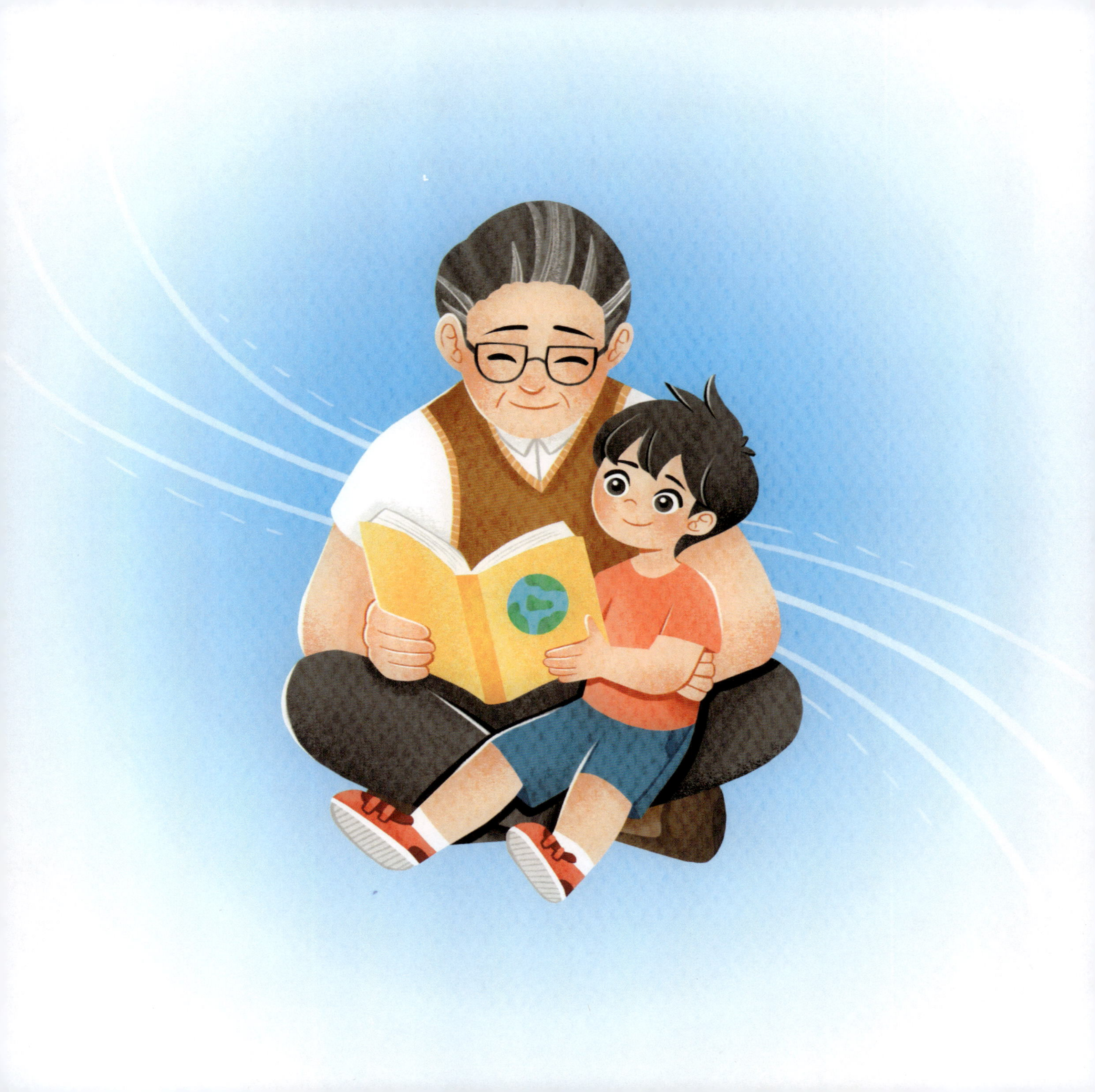

My grandpa is the best grandpa in the whole world.

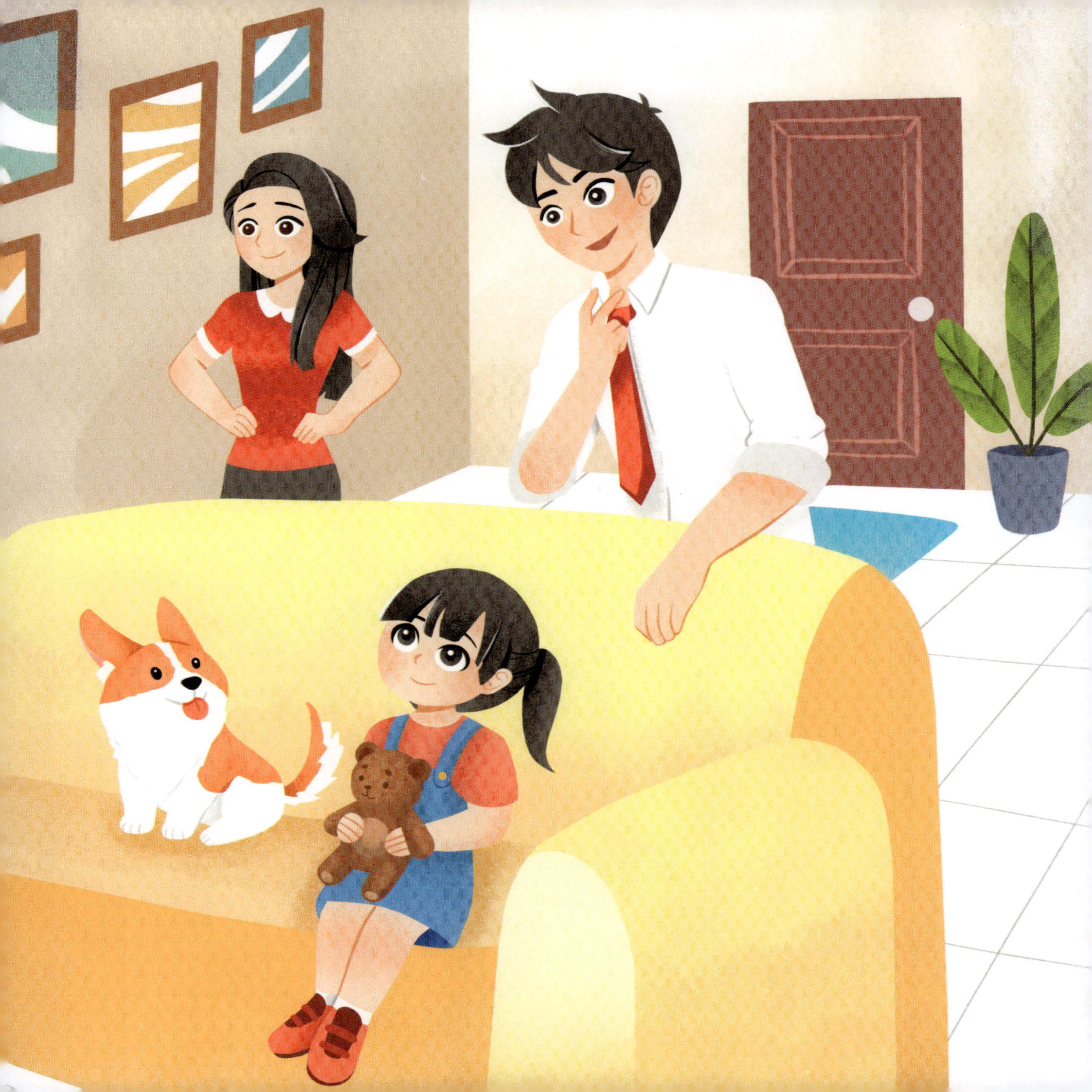

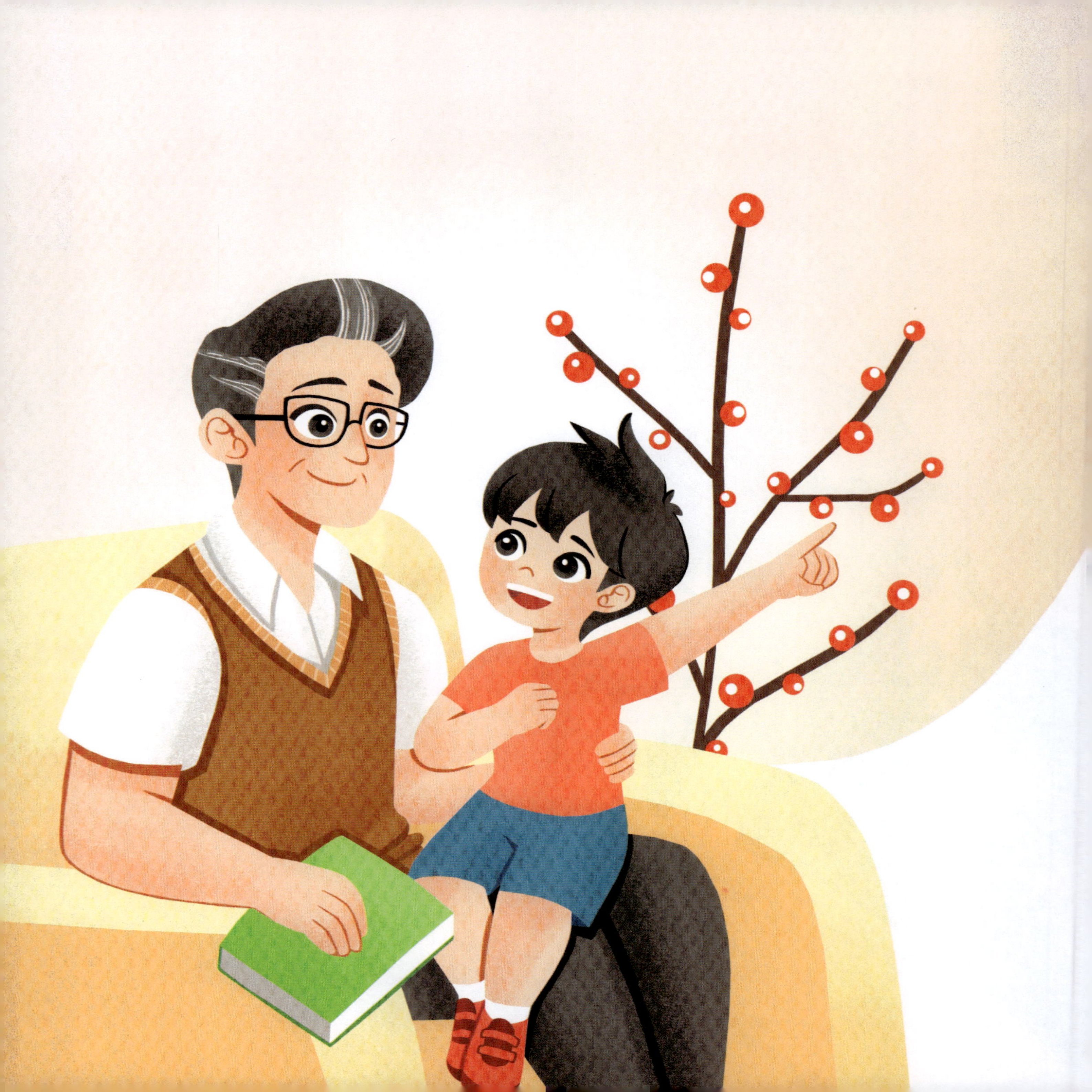

Even when he is busy,
he always makes time for me.

My grandpa grows delicious fruit and vegetables in his garden.

MAX

Max thinks they are delicious too!

Like me, my grandpa doesn't mind getting dirty...

My mum doesn't feel the same way though!

My grandpa knows the best jokes...

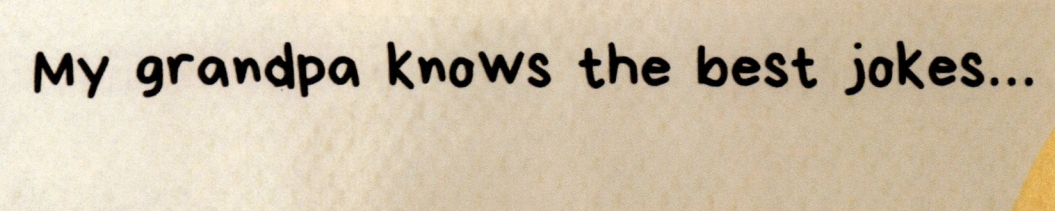

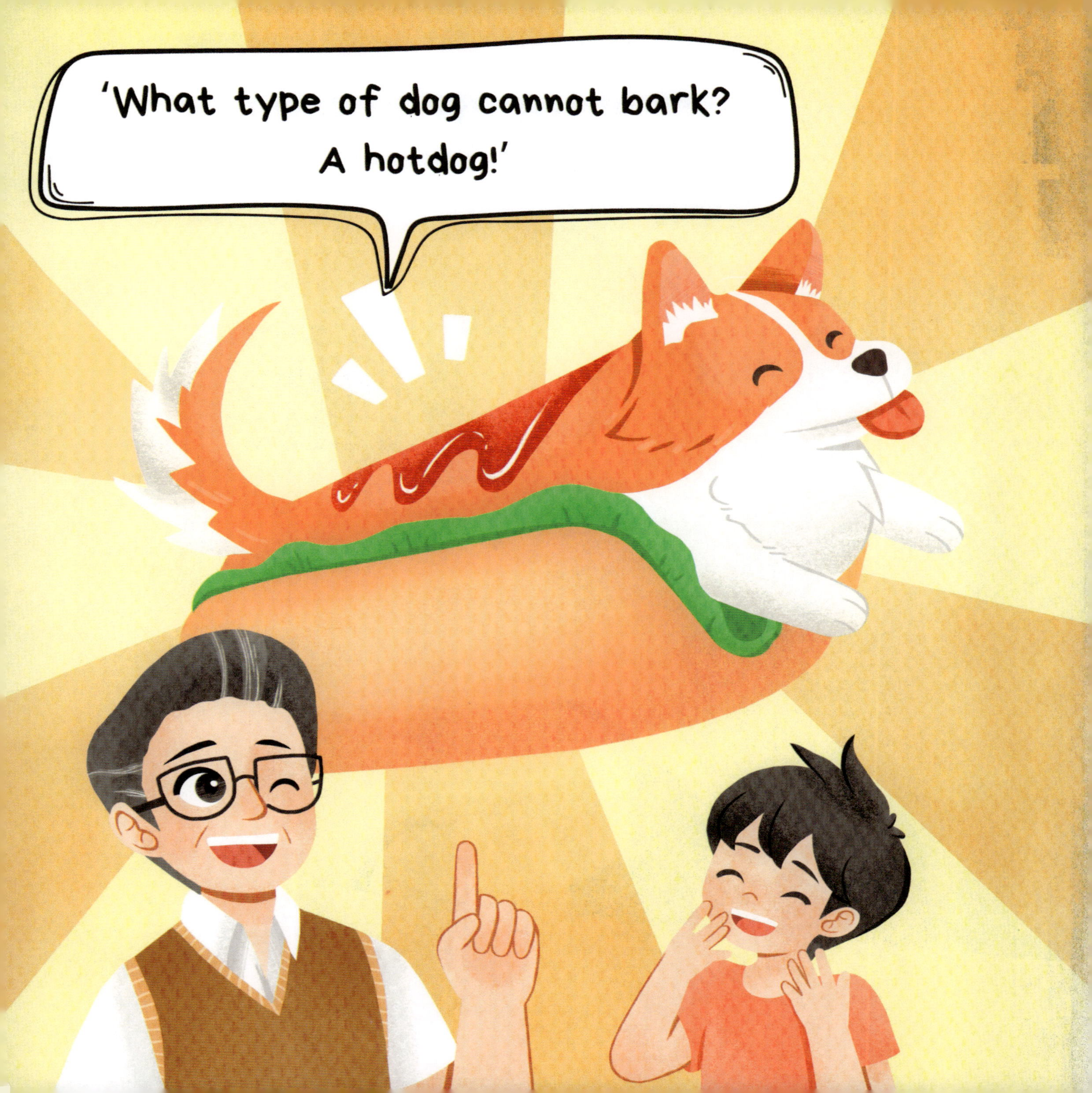
'What type of dog cannot bark?
A hotdog!'

...and he tells the most interesting stories.

Can you believe he used to be a spy?

My favourite thing to do with my grandpa

is to eat dim sum together.

He introduces me to different types of dim sum...

...and always orders my favourites.

When I am with him, I feel as if I can fly.

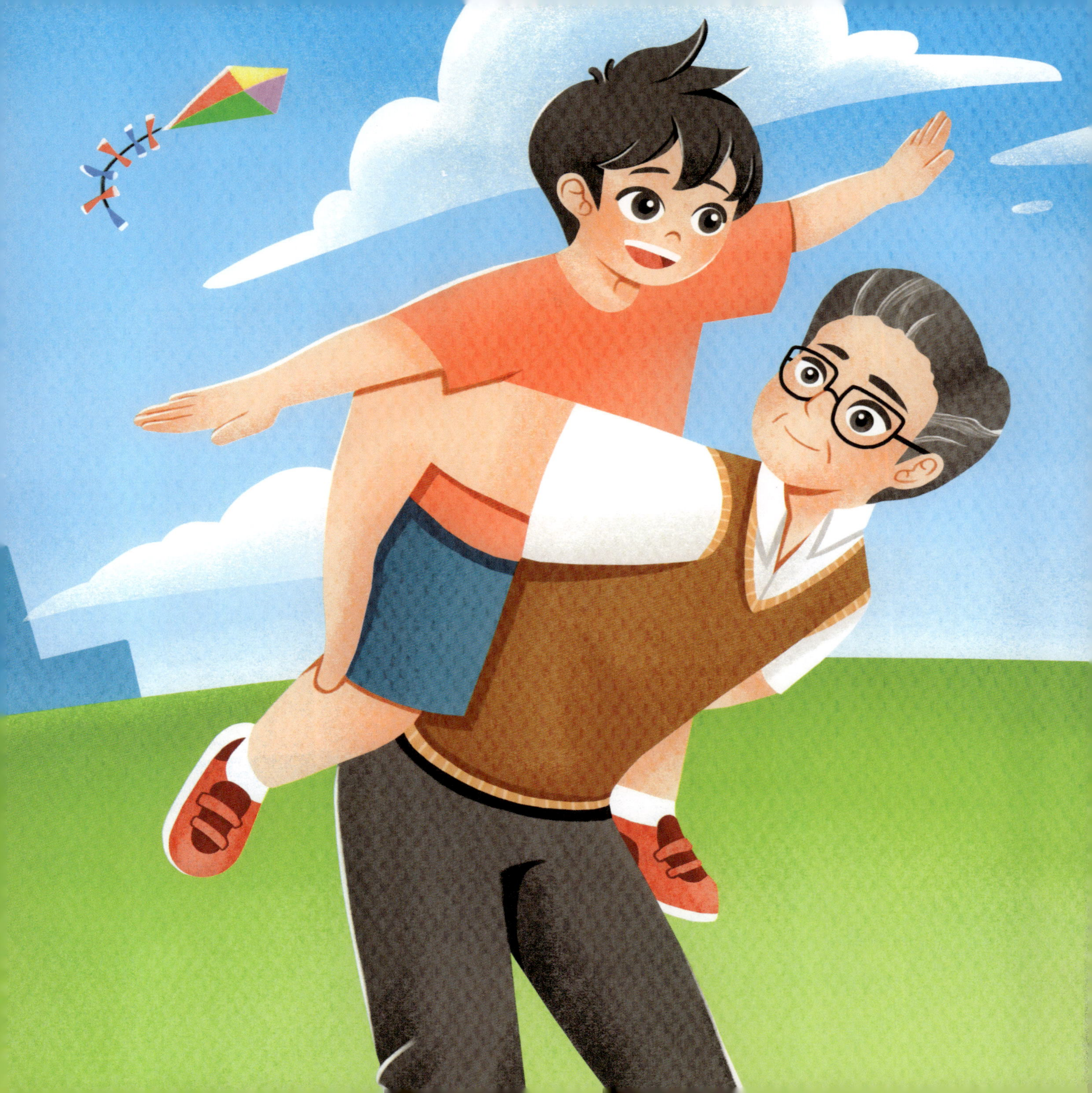

We travel the world together.

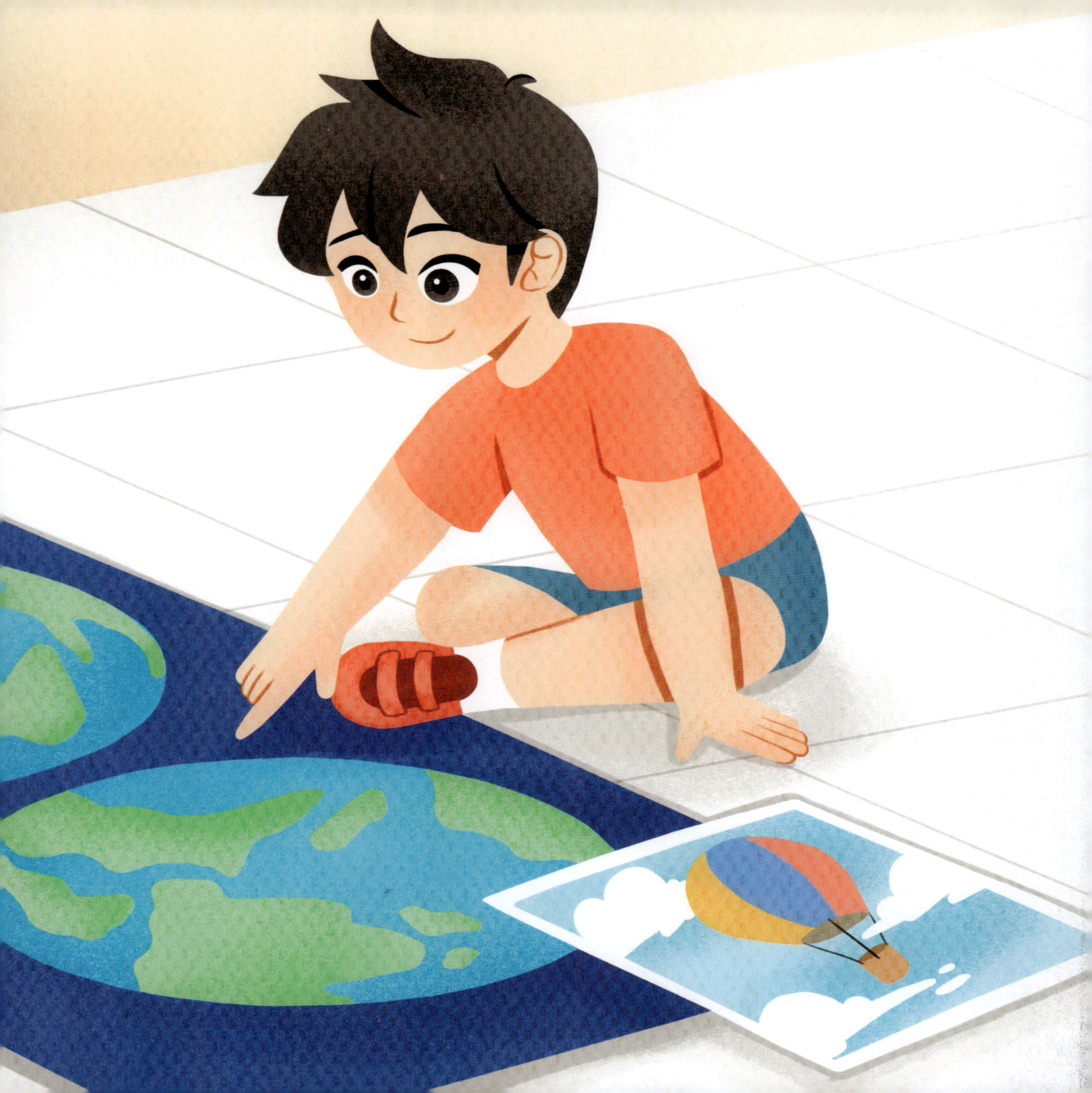

I am my grandpa's little helper.

I help him find his glasses...

...and teach him the latest trends.

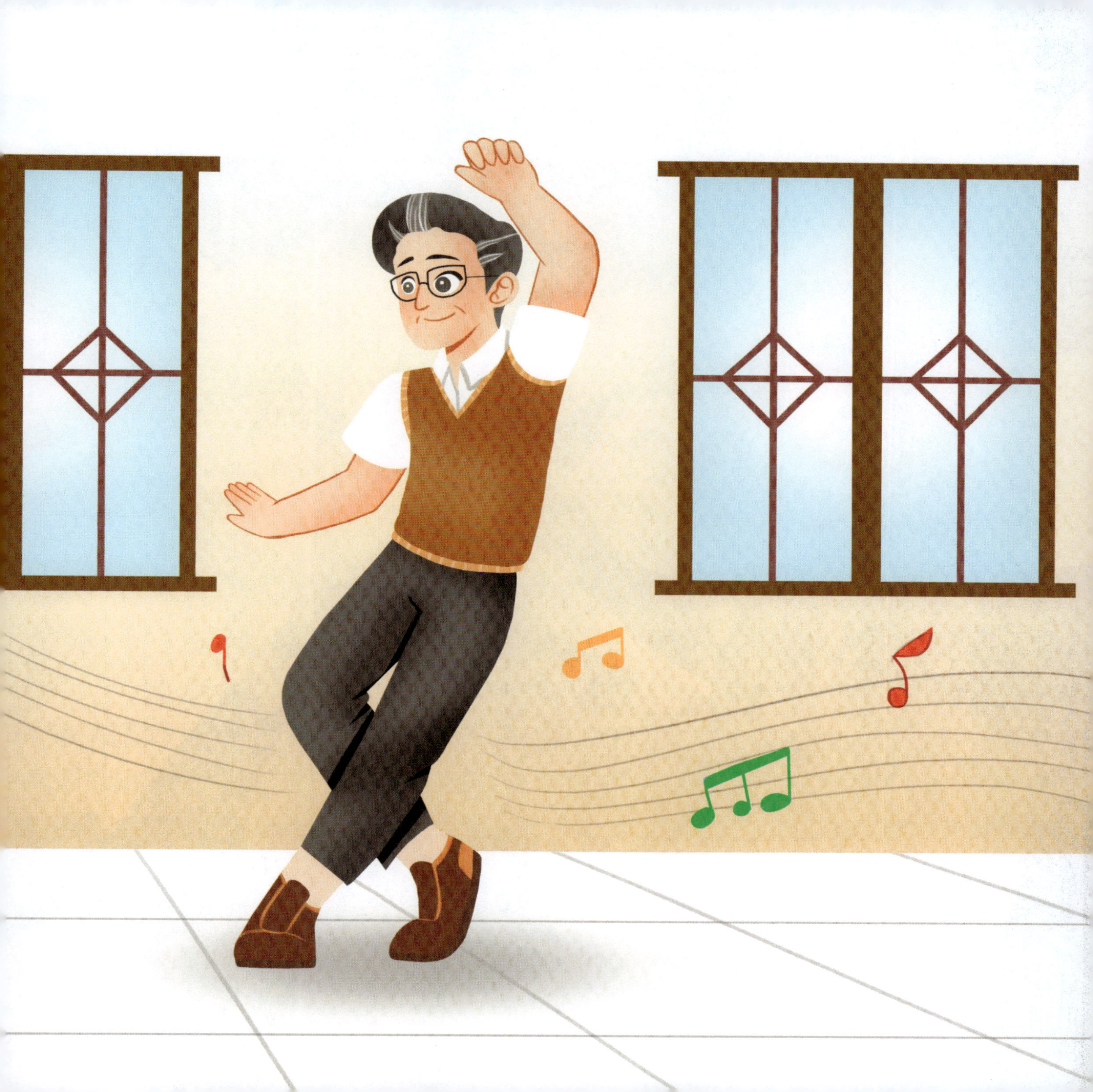

I love my grandpa.
He says I'll be taller
than him one day...

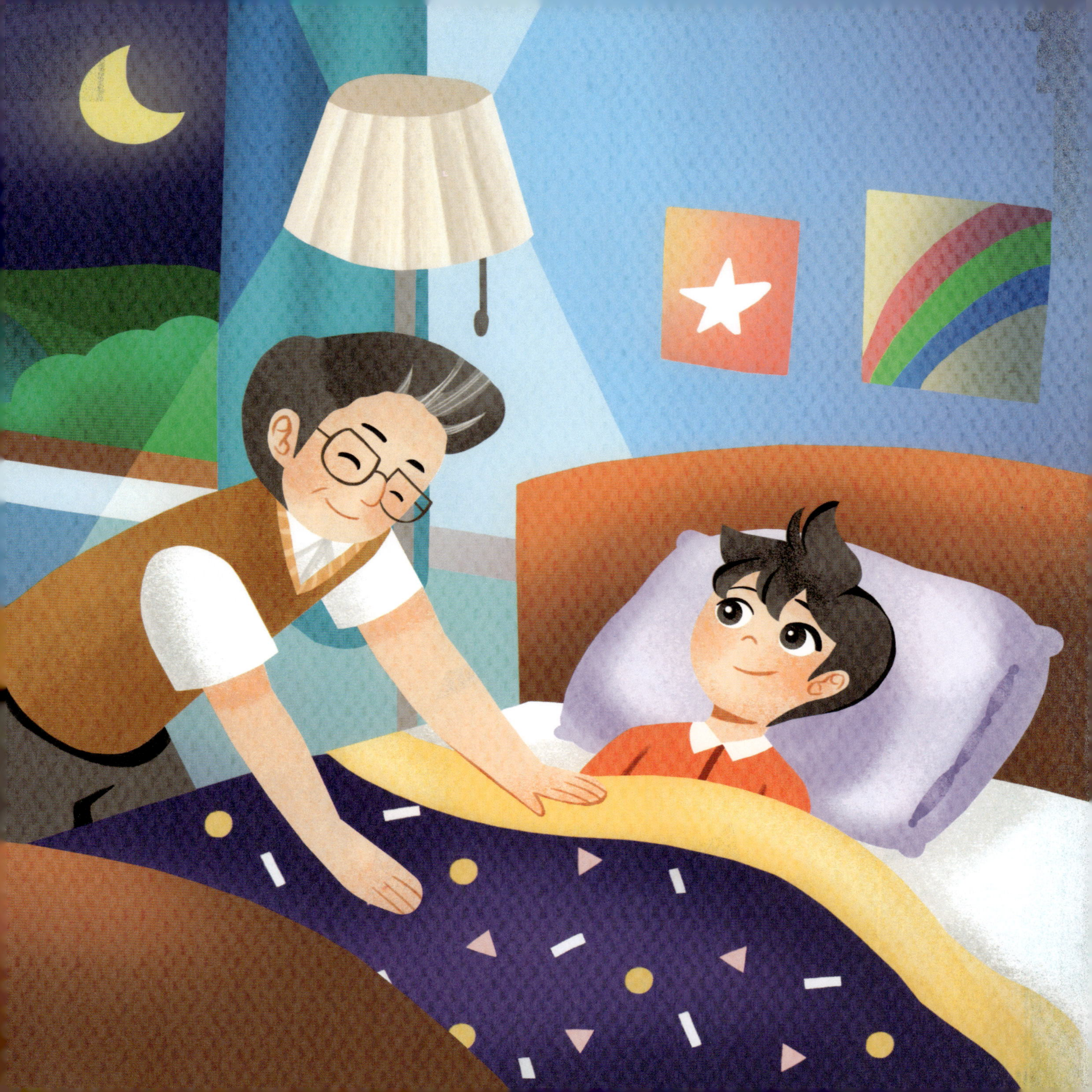

... but he will always be my hero.

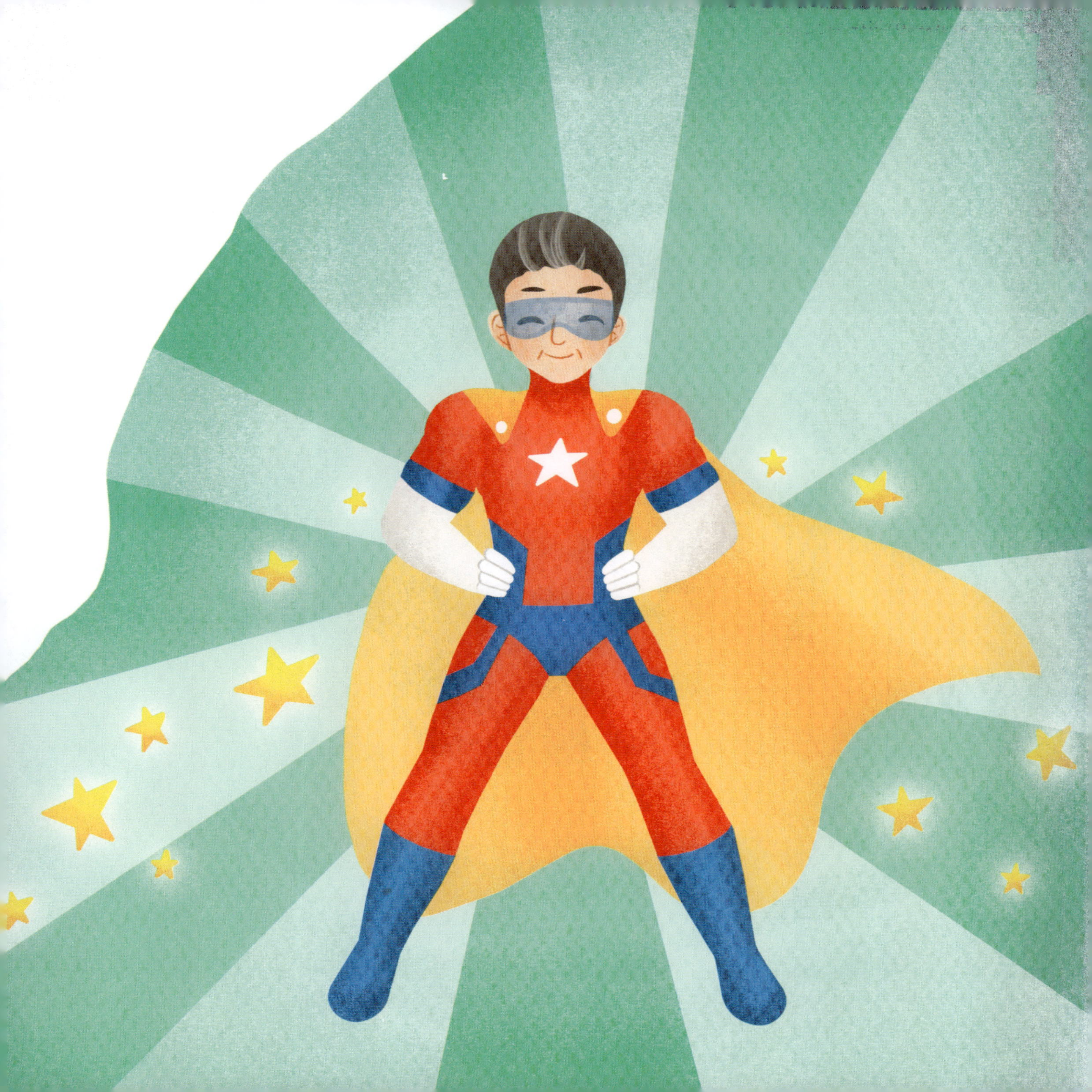

Printed in Great Britain
by Amazon